I0816538

KID CHEMISTRY LAB

BREAKING DOWN CHEMISTRY

Jessica Rusick

Checkerboard Library

An Imprint of Abdo Publishing
abdobooks.com

ABDOBOOKS.COM
Published by Abdo Publishing, a division of ABDO, PO Box 398166, Minneapolis, Minnesota 55439.

Printed in the United States of America, North Mankato, Minnesota
052022
092022

Design and Production: Kelly Doudna, Mighty Media, Inc.
Editor: Liz Salzmann
Cover Photograph: SDI Productions/iStockphoto
Interior Photographs: Allen.G/Shutterstock Images, p. 19; fotohunter/Shutterstock Images, p. 5; Gorodenkoff/Shutterstock Images, p. 7; grayjay/Shutterstock Images, p. 23; honglouwawa/Shutterstock Images, p. 16; Jenson/Shutterstock Images, p. 25; julie deshaies/Shutterstock Images, pp. 12–13; Mighty Media, Inc., pp. 26, 27, 28, 29; Nasky/Shutterstock Images, p. 15; nikkytok/Shutterstock Images, p. 11; Science History Institute/Wikimedia Commons, p. 9; SDI Productions/iStockphoto, p. 17; Soloviova Liudmyla/Shutterstock Images, p. 21

Library of Congress Control Number: 2021970089

Publisher's Cataloging-in-Publication Data
Names: Rusick, Jessica, author.
Title: Breaking down chemistry / by Jessica Rusick.
Description: Minneapolis, Minnesota : Abdo Publishing, 2023 | Series: Kid chemistry lab | Includes online resources and index.
Identifiers: ISBN 9781532198984 (lib. bdg.) | ISBN 9781098272913 (ebook)
Subjects: LCSH: Chemistry--Juvenile literature. | Demulsification--Juvenile literature. | Chemical bonds--Cleavage--Juvenile literature. | Dissolution (Chemistry)--Juvenile literature. | Science projects--Juvenile literature.
Classification: DDC 540--dc23

CONTENTS

Chapter 1

WHAT IS CHEMISTRY?

Chemistry is the study of matter. Matter is anything that takes up space. You are made of matter, and so is everything around you. Chemists study what matter is made of, how it behaves, and how and why it changes into different forms.

Chemistry is everywhere in our daily lives. Have you washed dishes with dish soap? If so, you have seen chemistry in action! The chemicals in dish soap break down grease. The grease then mixes with water and is washed away.

Chemistry can help explain many everyday processes. How do our bodies **digest** food? Why do leaves turn colors in the fall? Why does ice become water when it melts? These are all processes that can be explained by chemistry.

Photosynthesis is a common chemical reaction in nature. It is how plants use the sun's energy to produce food so they can grow.

Chapter 2

CHEMISTRY BASICS

Chemists are scientists who study chemistry. There are several branches of study within chemistry. These include biochemistry and physical chemistry. Biochemists study chemicals and chemical processes in living things. Physical chemists study how chemical reactions work.

Chemistry has been used to invent important materials such as plastic, fertilizer, and medicines. Today, some chemists work to make these materials better and safer. Other chemists use chemistry to develop new products. Chemistry helps scientists measure pollution in the **environment**, learn how the human body works, preserve artwork, and more.

Medical researchers use chemistry to try to develop cures for diseases such as cancer.

Chapter 3

CHEMISTRY'S BEGINNINGS

For thousands of years, humans practiced an early form of chemistry called **alchemy**. Alchemists studied matter to learn how to transform it into valuable materials, **potions**, and medicines. Many alchemists' methods were not based in science. However, alchemists made discoveries that led to modern-day chemistry.

Modern chemistry became a field of study in the 1600s and 1700s. Irish scientist Robert Boyle is sometimes called the father of modern chemistry. In 1661, he wrote one of the first chemistry textbooks. He also developed the modern definition of an element. An element is a substance that can't be broken down into other substances.

Robert Boyle lived
from 1627 to 1691.

Chapter 4

ELEMENTS

All matter is made of elements. Each element has its own **characteristics**. Some elements are metals, such as iron. Others are gases, such as oxygen. Elements that don't have the characteristics of metal are called nonmetals. Carbon is a nonmetal element.

There are 118 known elements. Most are found in nature. Iron, for example, is found in rocks. It is used to make steel for buildings, bridges, and tools. There is also iron in our blood. It helps carry oxygen throughout our bodies.

Every element known to scientists is listed on the periodic table of elements. Each element on the table is represented by one or two letters. This is the element's chemical symbol. For example, the chemical symbol for oxygen is the letter *O*.

Some elements do not exist naturally. Scientists create them in laboratories. One of these is americium. It is often used in smoke detectors.

Elements are made of small bits of matter called atoms. Atoms contain smaller units called **protons**, **neutrons**, and electrons. All atoms in an element have the same number of protons. Every **hydrogen** atom, for example, has one proton. Every oxygen atom has eight protons.

The number of protons an atom has is called an atomic number. An element's atomic number determines its **characteristics** and how it interacts with other elements. On the periodic table, elements are arranged in order of their atomic numbers.

PERIODIC TABLE

- Nonmetal
- Alkali metal
- Alkaline earth metal
- Transition metal
- Metal
- Metalloid
- Halogen

1 H HYDROGEN 1.0079								
3 Li LITHIUM 6.941	4 Be BERYLLIUM 9.0122							
11 Na SODIUM 22.989	12 Mg MAGNESIUM 24.305							
19 K POTASSIUM 39.098	20 Ca CALCIUM 40.078	21 Sc SCANDIUM 44.955	22 Ti TITANIUM 47.867	23 V VANADIUM 50.9415	24 Cr CHROMIUM 51.9961	25 Mn MANGANESE 54.938	26 Fe IRON 55.845	27 Co COBALT 58.933
37 Rb RUBIDIUM 85.467	38 Sr STRONTIUM 87.62	39 Y YTTRIUM 88.9058	40 Zr ZICRONIUM 91.224	41 Nb NIOBIUM 92.9063	42 Mo MOLYBDENUM 95.95	43 Tc TECHNETIUM (98)	44 Ru RUTHENIUM 101.07	45 Rh RHODIUM 102.90
55 Cs CAESIUM 132.905	56 Ba BARIUM 137.327	57-71*	72 Hf HAFNIUM 178.49	73 Ta TANTALUM 180.94	74 W TUNGSTEN 183.84	75 Re RHENIUM 186.207	76 Os OSMIUM 190.23	77 Ir IRIDIUM 192.217
87 Fr FRANCIUM (223)	88 Ra RADIUM (226)	89-103**	104 Rf RUTHERFORDIUM (267)	105 Db DUBNIUM (268)	106 Sg SEABORGIUM (271)	107 Bh BOHRIUM (272)	108 Hs HASSIUM (270)	109 Mt MEITNERIUM (276)

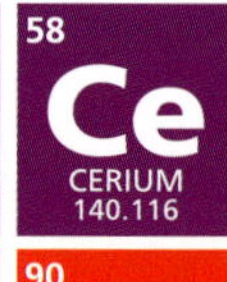

*	57 La LANTHANUM 138.90	58 Ce CERIUM 140.116	59 Pr PRASEODYMIUM 140.90	60 Nd NEODYMIUM 144.242	61 Pm PROMETHIUM (145)	62 Sm SAMARIUM 150.36	63 Eu EUROPIUM 151.964
**	89 Ac ACTINIUM (227)	90 Th THORIUM 232.0377	90 Pa PROTACTINIUM 231.03	92 U URANIUM 238.02	93 Np NEPTUNIUM (237)	94 Pu PLUTONIUM (244)	95 Am AMERICIUM (243)

The periodic table is often shown with each type of element a different color.

OF THE ELEMENTS

- Noble gas
- Actinide
- Lanthanide

								 2 He HELIUM 4.0026
			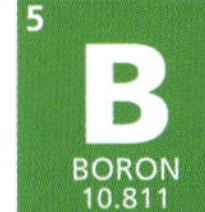 5 B BORON 10.811	 6 C CARBON 12.011	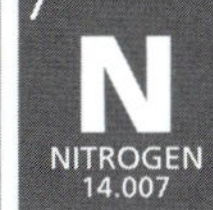 7 N NITROGEN 14.007	 8 O OXYGEN 15.999	 9 F FLUORINE 18.998	 10 Ne NEON 20.1797
			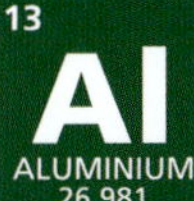 13 Al ALUMINIUM 26.981	 14 Si SILICON 28.085	 15 P PHOSPHORUS 30.974	 16 S SULFUR 32.066	 17 Cl CHLORINE 35.453	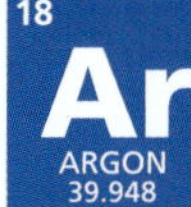 18 Ar ARGON 39.948
28 Ni NICKEL 58.6934	 29 Cu COPPER 63.546	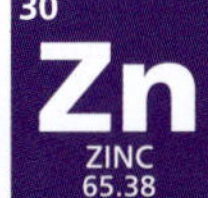 30 Zn ZINC 65.38	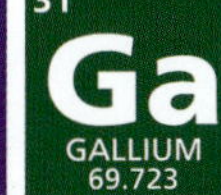 31 Ga GALLIUM 69.723	 32 Ge GERMANIUM 72.63	 33 As ARSENIC 74.921	 34 Se SELENIUM 78.971	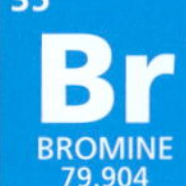 35 Br BROMINE 79.904	 36 Kr KRYPTON 83.798
46 Pd PALLADIUM 106.42	 47 Ag SILVER 107.8682	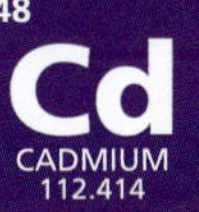 48 Cd CADMIUM 112.414	 49 In INDIUM 114.818	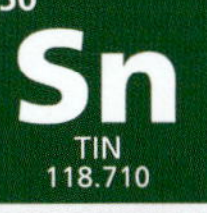 50 Sn TIN 118.710	 51 Sb ANTIMONY 121.760	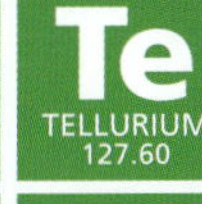 52 Te TELLURIUM 127.60	 53 I IODINE 126.90	 54 Xe XENON 131.293
78 Pt PLATINUM 195.084	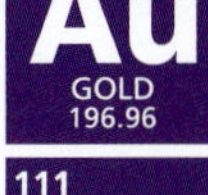 79 Au GOLD 196.96	 80 Hg MERCURY 200.59	 81 Tl THALLIUM 204.38	  82 Pb LEAD 207.2	 83 Bi BISMUTH 208.98	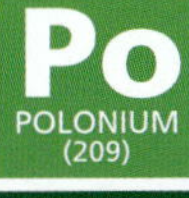 84 Po POLONIUM (209)	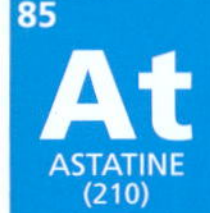 85 At ASTATINE (210)	 86 Rn RADON (222)
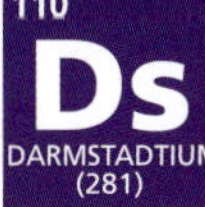 110 Ds DARMSTADTIUM (281)	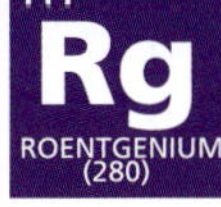 111 Rg ROENTGENIUM (280)	 112 Cn COPERNICIUM (285)	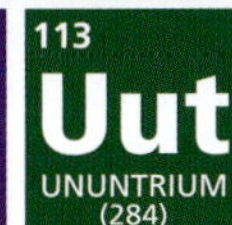 113 Uut UNUNTRIUM (284)	 114 Fl FLEROVIUM (289)	 115 Uup UNUNPENTIUM (288)	 116 Lv LIVERMORIUM (293)	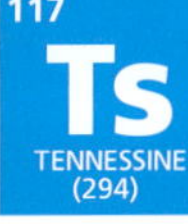 117 Ts TENNESSINE (294)	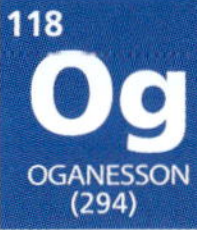 118 Og OGANESSON (294)

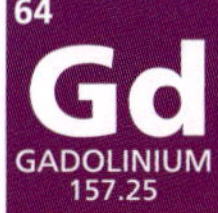 64 Gd GADOLINIUM 157.25	 65 Tb TERIBIUM 158.92	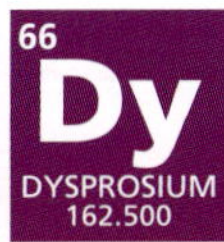 66 Dy DYSPROSIUM 162.500	 67 Ho HOLMIUM 164.93	 68 Er ERBIUM 167.259	 69 Tm THULIUM 168.93	 70 Yb YTTERBIUM 173.054	71 Lu LUTETIUM 174.9668
 96 Cm CURIUM (247)	 97 Bk BERKELIUM (247)	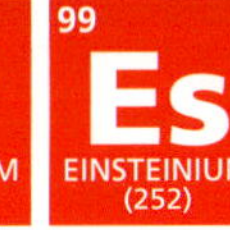 98 Cf CALIFORNIUM (251)	 99 Es EINSTEINIUM (252)	 100 Fm FERMIUM (257)	 101 Md MENDELEVIUM (258)	 102 No NOBELIUM (259)	103 Lr LAWRENCIUM (262)

Chapter 5

MOLECULES

Atoms bond together to form new substances. These new substances are called molecules. Atoms bond when their electrons interact in certain ways. The number of electrons an atom has determines what kinds of molecules it will make.

Some molecules contain atoms of different elements. These are known as compounds. Molecules have different **characteristics** than the original atoms. For example, **hydrogen** and oxygen are gases. But when two hydrogen atoms bond with one oxygen atom, the result is water.

Other molecules form when atoms of the same element bond. Three oxygen atoms combine to form ozone gas. In the atmosphere, ozone is one of the gases that protect Earth. It absorbs harmful rays from the sun. On the ground, ozone causes air pollution.

ATOMIC STRUCTURE

The center of an atom is called the nucleus. It contains the **protons** and **neutrons**. The electrons move around the nucleus.

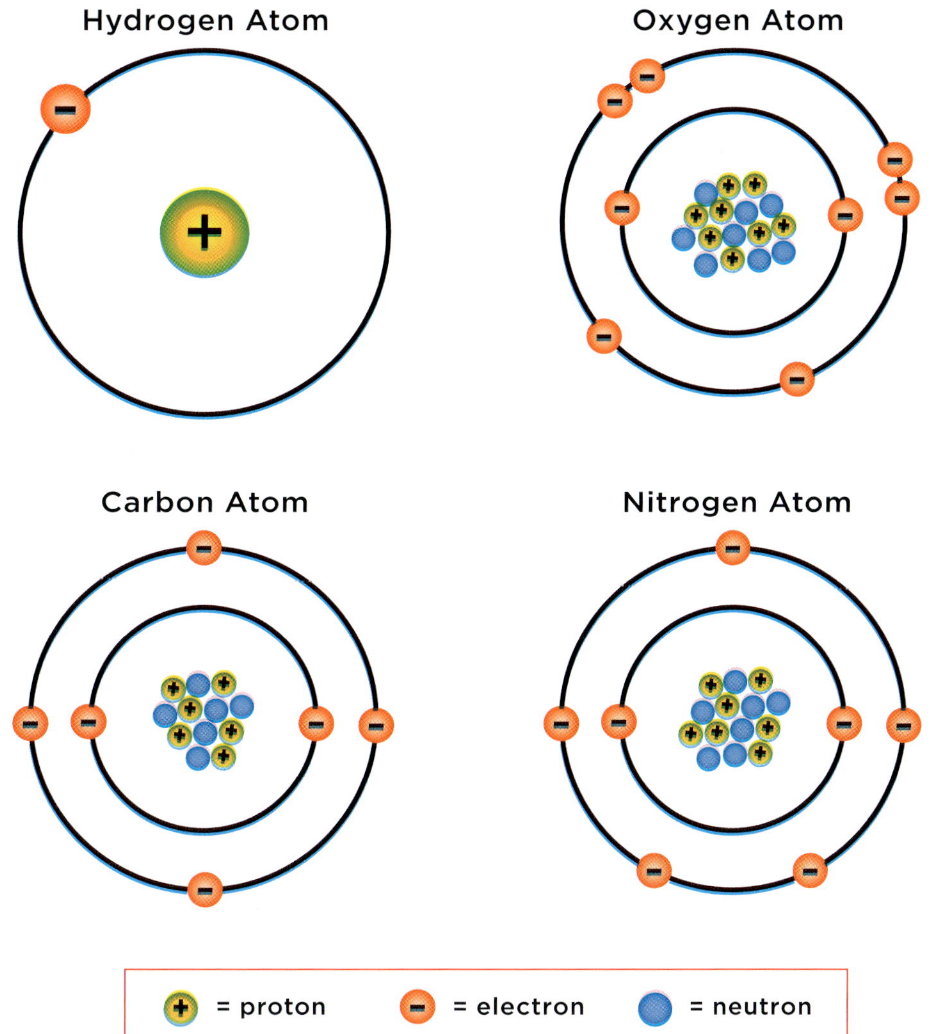

Molecules are written as chemical **formulas** using chemical symbols. **Subscript** numbers indicate how many atoms of each element there are in the molecule. The formula for a molecule of water is H_2O. The formula for ozone is O_3.

GREENHOUSE GAS MOLECULES

The gases in the atmosphere that protect Earth from the sun are called greenhouse gases. The main greenhouse gases are water vapor, **carbon dioxide**, methane, nitrous oxide, and ozone.

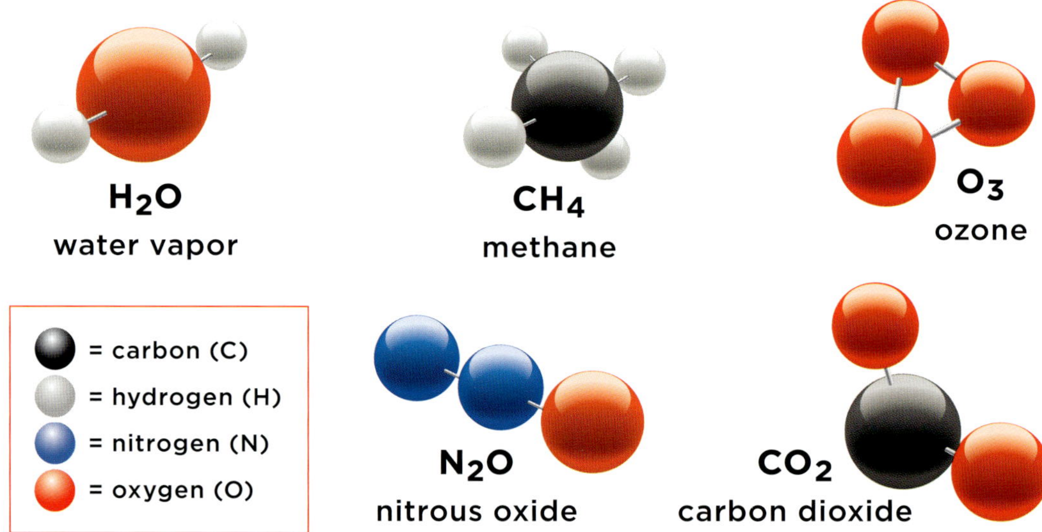

Models of molecules use different-colored balls for the different elements. Each ball represents one atom.

Chapter 6

CHEMICAL REACTIONS

When elements and molecules combine to form new substances, it is called a chemical reaction. A chemical reaction rearranges the atoms in a substance. This changes what a substance is.

The original substances in a chemical reaction are called reactants. The substances they produce are called products. For example, **hydrogen** and oxygen combining to form water is a chemical reaction. Hydrogen and oxygen are the reactants. Water is the product of the reaction.

There are several types of chemical reactions. The formation of water is a **synthesis** reaction. This is when reactants combine to make a product. Another type of reaction is **decomposition**. This is when reactants break apart to form two or more products.

Sometimes cities have thick, smoky air called smog over them. One type of smog is created in a photochemical reaction. This is when sunlight causes a reaction between some of the chemicals released by car exhaust and factories.

Some chemical reactions occur as soon as reactants come into contact. Other reactions require light, heat, or another factor for the reaction to occur. **Combustion**, or burning, is a chemical reaction that requires heat.

Many chemical reactions are impossible to reverse. Once you burn something, you can't unburn it! Some chemical reactions can be reversed with another chemical reaction. For example, a **synthesis** reaction may sometimes be reversed with a **decomposition** reaction.

Chemical reactions that produce heat, such as burning wood in a campfire, are called exothermic reactions. ►

Chapter 7

PHYSICAL CHANGES & MIXTURES

Chemical reactions are chemical changes. Matter can also undergo physical changes. A physical change affects how a substance looks. But it doesn't change what it is made of. Physical changes include cutting, crushing, and mixing. Many physical changes are reversible. If you crush a ball of clay, for example, you can easily mold it back into a ball.

Phase changes are also physical changes. A phase is a state of matter. The three main states of matter are solid, liquid, and gas. When an ice cube melts, it changes from solid ice to liquid water. This is a phase change. The ice and water may look different, but they are both made of water molecules.

STATES OF MATTER

A phase change affects how a substance's molecules are arranged.

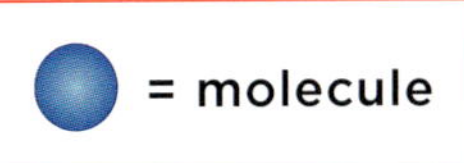

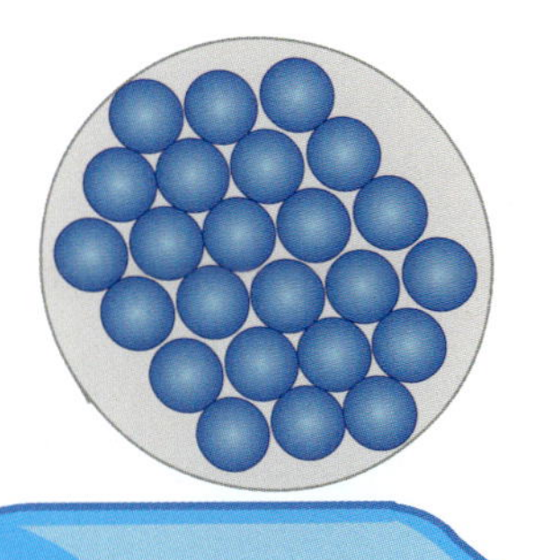

SOLID

Molecules are packed tightly together and can't move.

GAS

Molecules are far apart and can move around freely.

LIQUID

Molecules are packed loosely and can move a little.

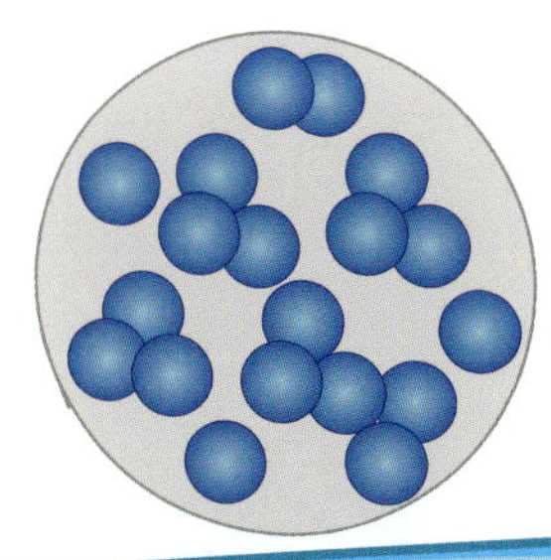

A physical change caused by combining two or more materials is a mixture. There are two types of mixtures. A **homogeneous** mixture is uniform, or the same throughout. Saltwater is a homogeneous mixture because salt is **distributed** evenly throughout the water. A homogeneous mixture is also called a solution.

A **heterogeneous** mixture is not uniform. A chocolate chip cookie is a heterogeneous mixture. Some areas of the cookie have chocolate chips, but others do not. So, the mixture is not the same throughout.

Steel is a homogeneous mixture of iron and carbon. Many everyday objects are made of steel, including cars and the machines that build them. ▶

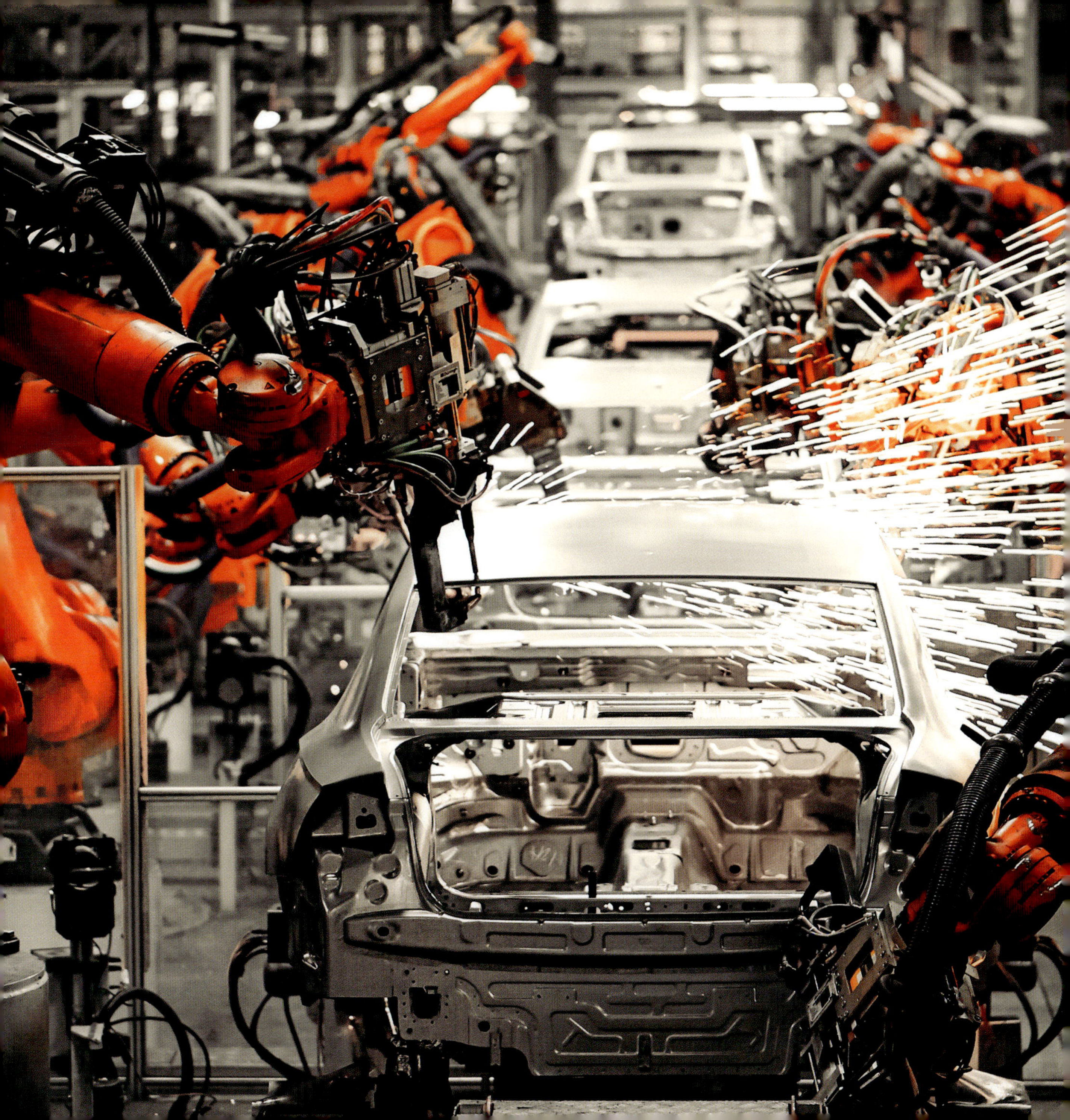

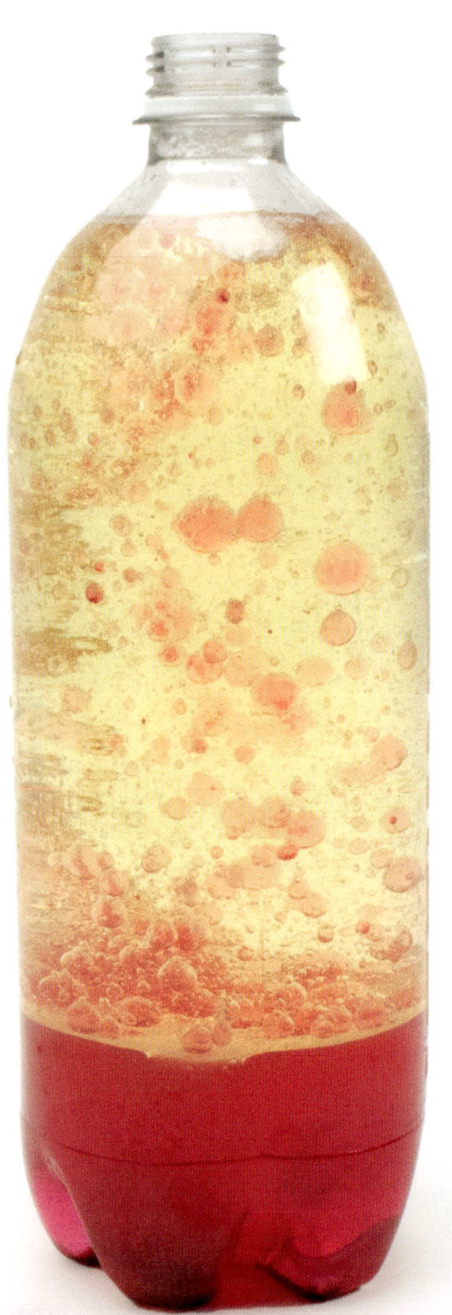

BUBBLE BOTTLE

WHAT HAPPENS

Oil molecules and water molecules do not bond with one another. So, they form two separate layers. Water's atoms are packed together more tightly than those in oil. This makes the water heavier than the oil, so it forms the bottom layer. The tablet **dissolves** in the water. This chemical reaction releases **carbon dioxide** gas. The gas carries water up through the oil. Then the gas escapes out of the top of the bottle and the water sinks back down.

EXPERIMENT!

Does the water temperature affect the reaction? What happens if you put the cap on the bottle? Experiment and record your results!

MATERIALS

- clear 2-liter bottle
- water
- measuring cup
- funnel
- vegetable oil
- food coloring
- **effervescent** tablet, such as Alka-Seltzer

STEPS

1 Pour 1½ cups of water into the bottle.

2 Add vegetable oil until the bottle is almost full.

3 Wait for the water and oil to settle into separate layers.

4 Add several drops of food coloring.

5 Break an effervescent tablet in half. Drop one half into the bottle. Watch the reaction!

THE SCIENTIFIC METHOD

Want to experiment like a real chemist? Follow the scientific method! The scientific method is a process scientists use to answer questions.

1. Ask a question. Research your question to learn more about it.
2. Develop a **hypothesis**. This is your best guess about the answer to your question.
3. Experiment to test your hypothesis. Record what happens during the experiment.
4. Review the results of your experiment to draw a conclusion. Was your hypothesis supported? Why or why not? Share your results with others.

FOAM EXPLOSION

WHAT HAPPENS

Hydrogen peroxide (H_2O_2) is a compound made of hydrogen and oxygen. Over time, it breaks down into water (H_2O) and oxygen (O). Yeast causes this **decomposition** chemical reaction to happen very fast. The oxygen is a gas that moves through the water, creating bubbles. The dish soap turns the bubbles into foam!

MATERIALS

- safety goggles
- plastic soda bottle
- plastic tub
- 3% hydrogen peroxide
- measuring cups & spoons
- food coloring
- dish soap
- mixing bowl & spoon
- 1 packet or 2¼ teaspoons dry yeast
- warm water

STEPS

1 Put on safety goggles. Place the bottle in a plastic tub. Have an adult pour ¾ cup of **hydrogen** peroxide into the bottle.

2 Add a few drops of food coloring to the bottle.

3 Add 1 tablespoon of dish soap to the bottle. Gently swish the bottle to mix the contents.

4 In a bowl, mix the dry yeast with 3 tablespoons of warm water.

5 Pour the yeast mixture into the bottle. Stand back!

EXPERIMENT!

What happens if you use a different amount of yeast? What about a stronger form of hydrogen peroxide? Experiment and record your results!

GLOSSARY

alchemy (AL-kem-ee)—a science that was used hundreds of years ago. Its main goal was to try to change ordinary metals into gold. Someone who studies or practices alchemy is an alchemist.

carbon dioxide—a heavy, colorless gas that is released when people and animals breathe out and produced when some fuels are burned.

characteristic—a quality or a feature of something.

combustion—the act or process of burning.

decomposition—the act of process of breaking down into simpler parts.

digest—to break down food into simpler substances the body can absorb.

dissolve—to pass into a solution or become liquid.

distributed—spread throughout.

effervescent—full of bubbles or able to form bubbles.

environment—nature and everything in it, such as the land, sea, and air.

formula—an expression that uses symbols to say what elements a substance is made of.

heterogeneous (het-uh-ruh-JEE-nee-uhs)—made up of parts that are different.

homogeneous (hoh-muh-JEE-nee-uhs)—of uniform structure or composition throughout.

hydrogen—the lightest chemical element. It is a gas with no smell or color and catches fire easily.

hypothesis (hye-PAH-thi-sis)—an unproven idea or theory based on known facts that leads to further study.

neutron—a small particle that has no electrical charge. It is part of the nucleus of all atoms except hydrogen atoms.

potion—a drink that is meant to have a special or magical effect on someone.

proton—a very small particle that has a positive charge. It is part of the nucleus of an atom.

subscript—a symbol, such as a letter or number, that is written slightly lower than the rest of the line of text.

synthesis—the production of a substance by combining other substances through a chemical process.

ONLINE RESOURCES

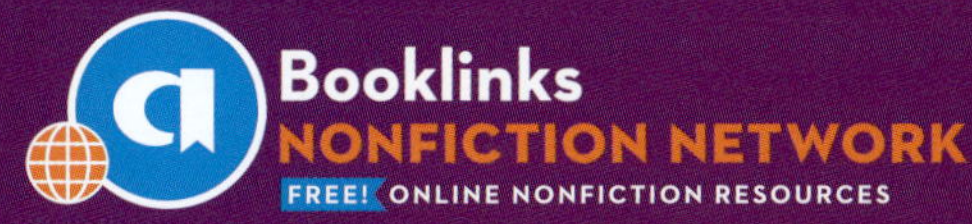

To learn more about chemistry, please visit **abdobooklinks.com** or scan this QR code. These links are routinely monitored and updated to provide the most current information available.

INDEX